ADAM LAZARUS

Adam Lazarus is an award-winning theatre creator, whose work has been showcased around the world. He is known for dynamic and implicating performances, including the international thought-disrupter *Daughter*; the radical race-oration *The Art of Building a Bunker* (co-written with Guillermo Verdecchia), and the vicious bouffon love play *Wonderland*.

Adam is an international instructor of performance who brings a dark and comic sensibility to his work and collaborations. He has acted as a creation director for countless actors, musicians, speakers, comedians, dancers and performance artists. He is a sessional acting instructor at the National Theatre School of Canada, Pig Iron Theatre's School for Performance, the Sibiu International Theatre Festival, and the University of Toronto. Adam was the founder and artistic director of the Toronto Festival of Clowns for ten years and is a graduate of and former apprentice to Master Teacher Philippe Gaulier.

Adam lives in Toronto, Canada, with his wife Sarah and their two children, Josephine and Oliver.

T0346946

Adam Lazarus

DAUGHTER

NICK HERN BOOKS

London

www.nickhernbooks.co.uk

A Nick Hern Book

Daughter first published in Great Britain in 2020 as a paperback original by Nick Hern Books Limited, The Glasshouse, 49a Goldhawk Road, London W12 8QP, in association with The Theatre Centre

Cover image by Alejandro Santiago

Designed and typeset by Nick Hern Books, London
Printed in Great Britain by Mimeo Ltd, Huntingdon, Cambridgeshire PE29 6XX

A CIP catalogue record for this book is available from the British Library

ISBN 978 1 84842 938 3

Foreword
Aislinn Rose

As a writer and performer, Adam Lazarus loves to live in the complicated. He's not interested in pat solutions or neat endings, and all that he asks of his audiences is that we sit in the complicated with him. He has built a career asking us to look at ugly things. I think it's fair to say that not many actors are willing to be hated by their audience, but in an effort to get us to look at the world, to really look at it in all its beauty and its gore, Adam offers himself up as the object and target of our hatred.

Daughter, as a play, as a performance, is often accused of trying to humanize a monster, but what I love about bouffon, the theatrical tradition from which Adam builds his performances, is that it so brilliantly reminds us of the monster in the human – the monster that's in each of us. It's when we can't acknowledge that, when we push it down and forget that it's there, when we deny this part of our humanity, we risk being overtaken by it.

Is the father in this story a monster?

So many have argued that he is, while I've spent hours in dozens of post-show conversations examining with audiences the hard truth that the father who loves to dance with his daughter, who cried over her birth, who loves his wife, is the same man we meet later in the show. Humans are complex creatures, or to paraphrase Whitman, we contain multitudes. We are both delicate and brutal. But the world becomes much simpler when we can neatly categorize people into groups of good and evil, human and monster, and even when we know better, we have a tendency to do just that. It's less complicated that way.

Bouffon, then, performs this essential service of tearing down those categories, of showing us the complications of human and monster, while turning a mirror on the audience and saying, 'Look at yourselves, this is you, this is us.' It's an uncomfortable position to find ourselves in: sitting in the dark with our fellow humans, and recognizing ourselves onstage. We feel the audience around us, ready to revolt against the man in front of us, the man we see ourselves in. And in our efforts to create distance from what we are seeing, we remind ourselves, it's just a play. He's just an actor.

And so what Adam does with *Daughter* is all the more extraordinary. By stripping away all of the traditional artifice of bouffon – the costumes and make-up, the grotesque characterizations and accents – and maintaining only that thing that is at the core of the form, the mirror, we are left staring only at our friend, our neighbour, our father, ourself.

Ourselves in the world we're truly living in.

We crave in those darkest of moments a view of a better world, of where we could be if we only worked harder, tried harder, addressed those darker parts of ourselves in a meaningful way. The bouffon might even show us a glimpse of something better, but it's also going to rip it away from us as quickly as it's offered. Why? Because that is not where we are. We are in the mess. We are in the complicated. We can't have catharsis because we haven't yet done the work.

So in the end, here we are in the dark, staring at the worst parts of ourselves, and in the case of *Daughter*, staring at the worst parts of the humans we encounter, and love, and support, and marry. Here we are in a world that holds those parts up and says, 'This is okay. Boys will, after all, be boys.'

And if we're bothered by this, if this is not okay, then what's to be done about it?

Daughter was co-created by Adam Lazarus, Ann-Marie Kerr, Melissa D'Agostino and Jivesh Parasram. It was developed and presented as a workshop production in August 2016 as part of the SummerWorks Performance Festival in Toronto, Canada. It was further workshopped when presented at the Sibiu International Theatre Festival in Sibiu, Romania, in June 2017, and received another workshop showing in Kingston, Ontario, Canada, as part of the Kick and Push Festival, August 2017.

Daughter premiered at The Theatre Centre in Toronto, Canada, on 9 November 2017 with the following artistic team:

Performer	Adam Lazarus
Director	Ann-Marie Kerr
Assistant Director	Melissa D'Agostino
Music and Sound Designer	Richard Feren
Lighting Designer	Michelle Ramsay
Stage Management	Rebecca Vandevelde
Producers	Tom Arthur Davis,
	Adam Lazarus,
	Jivesh Parasram,
	Aislinn Rose,
	The Theatre Centre,
	QuipTake,
	Pandemic Theatre

© Murdo Macleod

I'm Talking About You
Adam Lazarus

Satire must not be a kind of superfluous ill will, but ill will from a higher point of view… hatred against the bogged-down vileness of average man as against the possible heights that humanity might attain.

Paul Klee, *The Diaries of Paul Klee*

How many of you have had an affair or cheated on your partners? Spread an STI? Swore at your kid? Hit your kid? Punched a wall in front of your kid?

…

I don't need to know what your little secrets are. I know you have them. We all have secrets.

I am an artist and teacher, often known to work in a theatrical performance style called bouffon: a style rooted in the deep pleasure of mocking the human experience. Or we could call it the fine art of satire.

In the Middle Ages, throughout Europe, bouffons were the village outcasts, shunned and turned away from civil society and thereby forced to live on the outskirts of town. It was in these shantytowns, swamps and slums that the bouffons banded together and learned to love the freedom of a life beyond the system. They were uninhibited, unrestricted and uncontrolled. From time to time, they would hear stories from the village that had banished them. Stories about their queen's drug habit, her suitors, the king's problem with impotence, the banker's trysts with underage school girls. These tales of bad leaders made good fodder for the bouffons' plays. And bouffons like to make plays.

© *Bronwen Sharp*

Once a year, because of civic duty or royal pity, the village gentry would invite the bouffons back into town, to parade and put on a show. The plot of the show? Perhaps the zany tale of a backwards kingdom where a queen is high on amphetamines and has torrid affairs with her squires; where a king who can't get it up weeps for the plight of his wilting wiener; where a banker who is known to steal from the village poor plays dress-up in diapers while getting spanked by the high-school class president.

If the play was good, everyone laughed. If it was boring or offensive, the bouffon would be stoned to death in the town square. At least the town had entertainment!

When bouffon is effective, the audience is the target of the joke. But how to get away with making fun of the king? How does the Fool in *Lear* call him an idiot to his face and Lear laughs? This is the trick of the bouffon. They make us believe that the words they speak are inane, from the mind of madness or idiocy. Later, the effects of their words and images eat at our psyche. It is only after the curtain drops that we realize we were the subject of the mockery. That we are flawed. That we are implicated.

So, now that you've been exposed, what are you going to do? Apologize? Therapy? Suicide? Just asking.

Working in bouffon and satire, I have become increasingly interested in performing and watching difficult subject matter. I like having my nose stuck deep into the muck and left stuck there for a long while. I don't like things to be easy, because I don't think life is particularly easy. People are tricky. We are wonderful and capable of greatness, and at the same time we are defensive, scared, aggressive and mean. Anyone who says they are not these things is either lying or on the verge of a psychotic break...

My work has always examined a confusion of being, an in-between state of the human experience where civility meets chaos. In many of my shows, I approach satire through character: I wear costumes, I have accents, I speak words that sound like theatre-text. The target of the satire has included racists, classists, homophobes, Zionists, and, of course, left-leaning online-zine readers.

I think that I've been pulling my punches. Lately, I have come to believe that by dressing up as a character, I let my audiences off the hook. It's easier for an audience to have distance and not feel the full satirical barb if they are met with a character and asked to suspend their disbelief. For example, in one of my previous bouffon shows, *Wonderland*, I played the grotesque Eff, a charming piece of shit with no arms or legs, bound to a wheelchair and looking for love. I am not Eff and I'm almost one hundred per cent certain no one ever believed I was. The show had a big impact on many audience members... but I am curious what would happen if an audience thought they were watching the real me, the bouffon aspect of me, wielding a story that was plausible or at least familiar.

Daughter is an evolution of my bouffon work. You'll see me in jeans and a T-shirt telling stories that are true, and not true, and that delineation I will never tell. I want the audience to believe that they are hearing a real story. I want the audience to feel like they know me, that they are me, or that they are married to or dating me.

With *Daughter*, I am exploring how fucked up men can be, and being one of those men, I am reflecting aspects of my manly self that are hypocritical and nasty. It's a little scary and I think you may hate me. And that's okay. Judge me for the things I do and am. But, once the curtain falls, go home and parse out whether or not I was talking about you as well.

I am. Even you. Yeah, you. The one in the back, who firmly said no to the questions about affairs and abuse. We're all implicated in this one.

This was an article written for the online theatre magazine, Intermission (*www.intermissionmagazine.ca*)

© *Emma McIntyre*

Objective Violence
Rhiannon Collett

I'm watching Adam Lazarus punch an invisible girl in the face. Beside me, my former lover clenches his jaw. He shifts in his chair. I can practically smell his anxiety. The lights flash: I wonder if it's still snowing outside. I zone out, and when I come back, Adam's beating a guy with a fire poker. I've completely checked out. Dang, I think, I was really there before I could hear all the men in the theatre collectively wincing. You can't beat someone with a fire poker and not alienate yourself completely from at least part of an audience, can you?

Four years ago, I acquired a stalker. It was my first year of university – I was new to Montreal, I was trying to make friends and an unwell, socially inept man was trying to seduce me. He showed up at my work. He stared at me during classes. He watched me eat lunch. He followed me home. Even though I knew I was being stalked, I constantly second-guessed myself. I questioned my waves of fear, I ignored my sweaty palms.

The scariest part of being stalked by this man was not the act of being followed and watched, but the idea of what could happen if he decided to take things further. He never touched me, but his distant watchfulness became an 'objective violence,' a term coined by Žižek, paraphrased by Maggie Nelson, in her 2011 book, *The Art of Cruelty*, which was 'as invisible as dark matter, [a systemic violence] that underlies and mobilizes the structure of capitalism itself.'[1] My day-to-day existence became a prison I couldn't escape – by simply being physically present in the spaces I needed to be present in, I was immediately subjected to a touchless violence.

Daughter is full of objective violence – the casual misogyny, the nice dad gimmick, the normalized consumption of

---

1. Maggie Nelson, *The Art of Cruelty: A Reckoning* (W. W. Norton & Company, 2011, p 74)

pornography. It is a smart, agile show. But I have to wonder, if we removed all subjective (physical) violence from this piece, how would we speak about it? Would it just be a play about the everyman? Would it not still be violent?

'Žižek argues that one must always read explosions of subjective violence against this structural or objective violence, rather than remaining transfixed by the former... without such perspective, acts of subjective violences will nearly always seem in excess, monstrous, inexplicable, and – perhaps most dangerously... more horrifying than the structural violence that is their truer and more heinous cause.'[2]

It is when Lazarus's character snaps and moves into a world of violence 'with discernible agents and victims'[3] that the audience divides. There are those who are horrified by the physical assaults and those who saw the systemic violence from the get-go. The straight men are checking in – the queers, the women check out. I watch the people watching and think... I've already experienced worse without it touching my body.

Rhiannon Collett is a queer-identified playwright and performer whose work explores themes of misogyny, sexuality and ritual. Selected playwriting credits include Miranda & Dave Begin Again *(winner of the 2016 Playwrights Guild of Canada RBC Emerging Playwright Award);* Wasp *(commissioned by Nightswimming as a part of their 5x25 initiative); and* Tragic Queens *(commissioned and devised with CABAL Theatre, nominated for seven Montreal English Theatre Awards). Rhiannon lives in Toronto.*

---

2 and 3. Maggie Nelson, *The Art of Cruelty: A Reckoning* (W. W. Norton & Company, 2011, p 74)

Incremental Sins
Graham Isador

After watching *Daughter* for the first time I thought: that was a very well-done piece of theatre that I never want to see again. Four days later I purchased a ticket and was back in the audience. On opening night of the remount I'll be seeing it one more time. It's been over a year since the initial run and I'm still reckoning with my feelings about the piece. There are a lot of things that Adam's character says in the show that are completely offside... but also hilarious. Part of that is a byproduct of Adam's excellent timing and comedic chops, but if I'm being honest I've laughed at similar things from former bosses, shock jocks, and internet comments. Because it's all jokes, right? It's funny. No one actually believes those things.

The second half of *Daughter* goes to some pretty dark places. Each time I saw the show the audience (all of us) started with laughter that slowly died off throughout the run. Not many of us saw that second half coming but it's not hard to see how the show gets there. The little transgressions progress in a linear fashion until they're too big to be funny or brush off. It all feels worse because just a second ago we liked the guy. Adam. Sure, he was a bit of an asshole, but he was charming. So he gets a pass. You know, until he doesn't.

I'd like to say the reason I keep returning to *Daughter* is because the story, at least at its core, is about people I know. People that I worked with back when I was still in restaurants. People I've looked up to in the music scene or comedy. People in theatre. The show is a warning and a challenge on how to deal with them. But that's not the whole reason. Not really. The reason I keep coming back to *Daughter* is because it's a story about me. Not just my complacency but also my actions. All the different things I've done or failed to do. All the things that I've justified for one reason or another. Because of context. Or timing. Or whatever.

If you're paying attention I think this play should make you check your actions. *Daughter* gives you a context to do that. And it might make you uncomfortable to think of yourself that way, but you should. There is an old adage when talking about characters in pro-wrestling. The most successful wrestling personalities are just being themselves with the volume turned up to eleven. I've been thinking about that a lot in context to the play. So the guy on stage in the show isn't Adam, but it kind of is. At least in part. Just like the guy on stage isn't me, but it kind of is. At least in part. It's probably kind of you, too. Kind of.

And I think we all need to figure out what we want to do about that. I don't know. So I'll be watching the show again. I'll be thinking about it.

DAUGHTER

Why do men feel threatened by women?
They are afraid women will laugh at them.
Undercut their world view.
Why do women feel threatened by men?
They are afraid of being killed.

From an interview with Margaret Atwood

I become quite melancholy and deeply grieved to see men behave to each other as they do. Everywhere I find nothing but base flattery, injustice, self-interest, deceit and roguery. I cannot bear it any longer; I'm furious; and my intention is to break with all mankind.

Molière

I yam what's I yam. And tha's all what's I am.

Popeye The Sailor Man

For my kids

6

Character

THE FATHER

Setting

Daughter is a one-person show that takes place in this space, in this time. Although the play requires an enormous amount of physical acting, the performance-style is natural, and appears like stand-up or storytelling.

The audience enters the theatre. On the bare stage sits a stool. Upon the stool is a glass of water, and portable speaker attached to an iPod that plays Top 40 music for young girls – it's positive and fun. The lighting is bare and will not change for the first three-quarters of the play.

THE FATHER *walks onto the stage carrying a hula hoop. He is dressed dad-casual – sneakers, jeans, a hoodie – and wears butterfly wings, and a pink headband. He is gracious and kind. He places the hula hoop on the ground downstage centre, then stops the music.*

THE FATHER. This is my six-year-old daughter's playlist. We dance to this music. We have dance parties. And this is how she dances.

He pushes play. He's a pretty good dancer. Good hip-hop choreo. A little swag, a little bump and grind. A litte too much perhaps? He stops the music.

Just kidding, that's how I dance. She dances like this. She made this dance for me.

He pushes play. 'Girls' by Beyoncé. He dances a six-year-old child's dance routine with and around the hula hoop. He stops the music.

After she finished she said, 'Daddy, I'm so sorry. I made a few mistakes', and I said, 'No sweetheart. Everyone makes mistakes. Nobody's perfect.' And she said: 'No Daddy, everyone makes mistakes, so everyone's perfect.'

He rolls the hula hoop off.

She's awesome. And the number one song on her playlist is...

He pushes play. 'Everything is Awesome' by Tegan and Sara. He dances to song as both daughter and father, saying 'and I'm like, and she's like'. He stops the music.

But everything is not awesome. Right? Can we agree on that?

I said that to my daughter – not everything's awesome, right? And she said, 'Nope. Allergies, not awesome. When you're sick, not awesome. When you're about to die, not awesome.

When your eyebrows come off, not awesome. Monsters, not awesome.'

He flies wings offstage and takes off headband.

Bye-bye butterfly wings...

I would do *that* every second of every day with my daughter if I could, but I can't. I always think it's going to be one way with her, but it's something else. I mean, I love my daughter to bits, but from day one it's also been like – AH!!!!

Makes a sound and gesture of confusion/pain/frustration.

You know what I mean?

From the day she was born. October 2nd, 2013.[1] We planned on a natural childbirth... it didn't work out that way. We had a 'doula'. Does everyone know what that is?

Waits for an answer from the audience.

For those of you who don't know, a 'doula' isn't the same as a midwife. It's more like a birthing coach. So, a doula can't actually deliver the baby, but they teach you to feel positive about delivering the baby.

We were also a hypnobirthing couple. Are any of you hypnobirthing couples?

Waits for an answer from the audience.

Hypnobirthing is where the mom hypnotizes herself, goes inside, is *one* with her pain, and has what they say is a fuller experience of childbirth. It's very holistic. It didn't really do much for me...

But the Doula did teach us how to speak, like a new language. Like it's not called the bloody show, it's called the birth show, they're not called contractions, they're called surges, your water doesn't break, it releases, and it's not about being free from pain, but rather, free from fear.

Which was the name of the movie the doula showed us – *Free From Fear: A Hypnobirthing Journey.* In which, the

---

1. Depending when the show is performed, this date should change to keep the daughter's age at six years old.

starring role was a woman in labour, in a pool, in her den, and everyone's there – like her partner, and her toddler, and the doula, and the neighbours, and the dog. And she is spreadeagle! And every time a surge comes she says: 'Come, come. A surge is coming.' And then the dog like licks her hand, and she goes inside:

Mimics hypnobirthing – deep squat, eyes shut, light humming and focused.

'*Mmm. Mmm. Mmm…* That was intense.'

He mops his brow, pets the dog.

Now I don't know how many of you have had kids – but it's not like that.

But you know, hypnobirthing helped my wife: five, ten minutes a day, breathing, meditating, being present with her pregnancy. So, it was good for that. I tried it a couple of times, and I couldn't stop laughing. But I was happy that it worked for my wife.

When labour officially started, we spent the first seven hours at home. And my wife was doing hypnobirthing during contractions. I made her some toast that she couldn't eat. She took a bath, and I put the shower head on her belly, and she was like, 'Don't touch me'. We watched half of *Office Space* which is a shit movie.

The energy in the house was high and chaotic. And then the pain was too much, contractions seemed close together, so we got in the car to go to the hospital.

My wife and I and this enormous bag, which we called the doula duffle, filled with, like, everything. Like, I joined Costco[2] to fill that bag. I got a case of water, a case of Cool Blue Gatorade – my favourite – an extra-large bag of party mix potato chips, a camping mattress and a pillow in case I needed to take a nap, and a dozen underwear for my wife, extra-large, not white.

So, we get in the car, and we're driving to the hospital, and I

---

2. Costco is a big North American bulk store. Use equivalent.

remember it was ten-thirty at night and drizzling. And we get to the first intersection, and the light is red, and I look out the window – and there's the famous Canadian filmmaker Atom Egoyan[3], I kid you not! And I'm like, 'Oh my gosh it's Atom Egoyan!' And I go to do down the window, and the light turns green, but I do down the window anyway and the rain starts to come in and I look at my wife and she is breathing A LOT, kind of hunched over, holding the seat-belt, like, 'hhhhhuuuuuhhhhh'. And I'm thinking, 'But it's Atom Egoyan.' And I want to say, 'Hey Atom Egoyan! Hey man! I'm having a baby!' And I met him once at a party. And I feel like this will connect us for later! And then I look back at my wife and I'm like… 'No. Keep driving!'

He shakes his head in judgment of himself and mockingly pats himself on the back for a decision well made.

So, we get to the hospital and we are ready to have this baby. And then triage does an exam and we are NOT ready to have this baby. They say she's not really dilated, and she hasn't progressed enough. That's how they talk. In terms of progression. They say this baby isn't coming anytime soon, but they check us in anyway, and we go into the room where the baby will eventually be born. And I quickly set everything up – my camping mattress and pillow, and this iPod dock, which I also bought at Costco. I loaded up my iPod with four playlists for the 'birthing sequence': Pre-labour, hard labour, Top 50, and '*In the Glow*'. We didn't listen to one song.

And, I even put up this sign that I printed and laminated on the outside of the door which read, 'Please be mindfully quiet when entering, we are a hypnobirthing couple.'

Ten hours, and a whole lot of contractions later, still nothing.

Then at hour fourteen, I started to feel sick. Like sick to my stomach. Like you know that feeling when you're so tired you think you're gonna puke? Like that. So, I turn to the Doula and I say, 'Michelle, I am so tired. What should I do?' And she looks at me dead in the eyes and very cleanly says:

---

3. Atom Egoyan is an iconic Canadian director – feel free to choose an artist more relevant to your local community if desired.

'Get over it.'

I didn't know! It was a teaching moment. I didn't know. Do I nap now? Do I nap later? Do we like take shifts, Michelle? And I know this sounds fucked up, but, you know, my wife had labour keeping her awake. What did *I* have?

Dismisses his terrible joke.

I don't go to sleep. I don't go to sleep. But what I do do is, a few hours later, I go for this walk in the hall – And my wife is with the Doula – And I'm in the hall and I'm pacing back and forth with my hoodie up, like this…

He puts his hoodie up.

Which I do sometimes when I want to think. And some nurses are over there, and then the OB, the baby delivery doctor, she comes up to me, and she says: 'She's not progressing as much as we'd like, we're gonna break her water, does that sound good?' And I'm like, 'Um I don't know. What do you think?' And she looks up to my face and goes 'Oh I'm sorry, I thought by the way you were dressed that you were a nurse!' And I'm like, 'No. I'm the dad.' And she says, 'Ha! It's because of the greys… Anyway, we're going to break her water.'

Are you sure?

And she convinces us that we have no other option, and they do it. They break her water. And that's it. First intervention. And then they hook her up to a monitor and start monitoring everything – blood pressure, heart rate of baby, mama, everything. And this what they call *procedure* is now a potential liability.

And then labour gets really fucking painful for my wife. And it's hour twenty-two and she's still not dilated and she's still not progressing, and she asks for an epidural.

Beat.

And we'd talked about this. Like the whole thing about the hypnobirthing thing, because the Doula she warned us that once you have one intervention, the hospital's all up in it and boom, boom, boom: C-section.

But she needs it, so we do it.

And it's the one part of the labour that I can't watch because they say if she moves while the needle is being put in, there is a chance that she could become paralyzed. But you won't know for two weeks. And they ask me if I want to hold her while they do it. And I'm like no, I don't want to hold my wife, I don't trust myself.

So, she's draped over one of the nurses, and the anesthesiologist is behind her. And I can see her through my fingers and she's looking right at me. And they take this long, thin needle and they start to snake it up her spine. And she goes:

He flinches/shakes.

…and it's just so scary and unnatural and I don't understand anything.

And it doesn't work.

They do this ice test, where they put a pack of ice on your upper thigh and if you feel the ice it means the epidural didn't work, and my wife says, 'I feel the ice.' And the doctors say, 'No, you don't'. And she says, 'Yes I do'. And they're like, 'that's weird.' So they do another exam, and they discover that the baby is spine-on-spine. Which is very painful for mum every time she has a contraction.

And the doctor says, 'Ah! That's why! Okay. Let's do a C-section.' Boom, boom, boom.

Now my wife and I, we pledged to each other to be happy, whatever the story. We're getting a kid out of this in the end. C-section, episiotomy, whatever. We bring a baby home. But I hear those words C-section, and I feel like a failure. So I ask my wife what she thinks and she says, 'I don't care anymore. I'm just so tired.'

And suddenly it's on me. And I spend some time looking at her. Kind of staring, judging, confused, angry, scared.

And then I remember the doula saying, if this happens, ask the doctors what happens if we wait? So I do. I ask the doctors, 'What happens if we wait?'

And the water breaker one says, 'You have an hour to turn that baby around and if you can't, I'm cutting it out.'

That's how they fucking talk.

He takes hoodie down.

So the doctors they leave and my wife gets on all-fours, and starts doing yoga. Like cat and cow to make room for the baby to spin. And the pain is so intense that she's passing out in between contractions. And the contractions are about two minutes apart, one minute in length, and fawking painful.

So my wife is over the bed, or the gurney or whatever it's called and she's passing out in between contractions and when she wakes up she screams and does yoga while she's screaming.

It's like this:

He embodies and verbalizes a long and agonizing contraction. He does not mock this experience – it is performed with empathy and love.

And I'm like, 'Oh my god this is happening!' And I'm there, I'm yelling in her fuckin' face every step of the way and she's yelling in mine.

It's like, it's like, you know those movies you know when women are giving birth and they're like, 'Ooohh ouchy! Ouchy!' It is nothing like that! I mean go online and google '*real birth*'. Or actually don't. Don't. Just wait. For it to happen to you. Live. And if that's not your thing, then ask a friend if you can go watch.

Beat.

So about an hour later, the doctors come back in, and they do another examination and they discover that the baby has turned. And everyone starts crying because we're so happy. And...

I'm lying. Nobody is crying. We're just all really happy. Well *I'm* really happy. I'm not sure about everyone else and my wife is still having contractions. And she asks for another epidural, and this time it works. And she turns to the anesthesiologist and says: 'I love you.' And passes out.

And I go get a burger.

And then I throw out the burger. 'Cause I'm like, 'Wait, my breath is going to smell like pickles and onions while she's pushing.' So I get a smoothie.

And I go back into the delivery room and enter what feels like the eye of the storm. It's calm. And I drink my smoothie. And I go to the bathroom and I take a picture of myself in the mirror. Because I will never be that man again.

Silence.

When I come back into the room, you can see the intensity of the contractions on the monitor. And the next time the doctors come in, they wake her up and say, 'It's time. It's time for you to start pushing and show us what you're made of.'

And she sure as shit does.

For two hours she's pushing and opening and pushing and opening and... you have not seen strength like that, I mean, like the warrior of woman, you know? Like, I couldn't do that shit. And she pushes and opens and pushes and opens and one more push... and out comes my little girl.

And she's purple. And they immediately take her and they put her on a side table. She's purple. She's limp. And she looks dead.

So I ask the doctors, 'Is everything okay? Is this normal? Is she okay?'

And the doctors say, 'Sir, please back away.'

Okay.

'Babe? Are you okay? Is everything okay?'

She nods.

And the baby's not crying. Because the doctors won't let her. Because they think that she may have swallowed meconium, which is feces, while she was inside the womb, and if she breathes, it'll go in her lungs, and I think, 'Maybe when you broke her fucking water!'

Is she okay?
'Babe, are you okay?' (*Nods.*)

And she has no clue what is going on here.

And the doctors take a tube and they stick it down my little girl's newborn throat and they plunge a few times.

And I don't like this. I don't like it at all. Please.
'Babe? Are you okay?'
Please – just give me my baby – what about skin-on-skin?

And then… she starts crying. And the room breathes again. And the doctor says: 'Okay. Dad.' And they hand me the baby… and we have a daughter. I have a daughter. Holy shit! What does that even mean?

And for three years, I'm like that, 'Are you okay? Is everything okay? What does this even mean?'

And it's not until the birth of my second child, my son, that I go back and I think, 'Why couldn't I have just been okay?' My son was born at home, in my bed, inside the caul. Which means that he came out still inside of his waters. And the midwives said, we couldn't have asked for a smoother birth. And they also say it's a sign. That a baby born inside the caul won't drown at sea. And it's the first telltale sign of the next Buddha. So my son could be the next Buddha. That's all I'm saying.

Everything was perfect for my boy. And from day one, I have been in a constant state of panic with my daughter.

Beat.

I yell at my daughter a lot.

I remember before I had kids, somebody said to me, 'One day you're going to see someone yelling at their kid, and you're going to judge them for it. And they're going to see you seeing them... and they're not going to care.'

And I swear it was the same day I heard that story: I was riding home on my bike and I passed this guy shoving his kid into the backseat of an SUV, and he was like – 'You get in that car and you sit down and you don't move!' And I rode past him, and he turned and looked right at me, and he saw me seeing him, and was like – 'I don't care about you and what you think because this thing over here is driving me nuts – Get in the CAR!'

Beat. Gesture of discomfort in his shoulder.

I have an injury. Right here. In my shoulder. From throwing my three-year-old daughter into her bed.

For two months straight, before my son was born, my daughter woke up seven times a night. For two months straight. And you go nuts. I went nuts.

He mimes the following:

And this one night, she kept coming out of her room, and on the sixth time I did this thing where I shoved her backwards, got in her face and said: 'Get in your room! If you come out of there one more time, there will be. There will be.' And I didn't know what there will be, but: 'There will be!' And she went back into her room... and thirty minutes later, at four thirty in the morning, she came out again and I went nuts. But with focus. I picked her up, I threw her into her bed, I got in her face and pushed down on her shoulders, driving her into the mattress.

The gesture is long and uncomfortable to watch. When it finishes, we see THE FATHER *retract, slightly diminish and then put back on his defence. He stands tall.*

It worked. She didn't come out again.

He looks at the audience and decides to proceed.

So, I want to know, are you okay that I did that? I'm asking. For real.

*Waits for answers from the audience. Listens to them.
Responds accordingly.*[4]

I hear some yeses and some nos. And a lot of silence.

'Cause I'm not sure if I'm okay that I did that. But I think
what's got to leave the room is this thinking of: *Well I
wouldn't have done it like that.* 'Cause man, I wouldn't have
done it like *that* either, now. I wouldn't have done a lot of
things. But I did. Like a lot of stupid shit. Haven't we all?

Waits for answer from the audience. Listens.[5]

A lot more yeses. And a lot of virtue.

Beat. He looks at the audience.

Throughout the rest of the play, THE FATHER *looks for
complicity in the audience. He interprets every laugh, gasp,
and silence as a reassurance that his point of view and
behaviour is correct.*

He decides to proceed.

---

4. Responses vary from hard absolutely nos to declarations of *I've done worse.*
There is always a lot of silence. It's easy to lose the audience here, so it is
important not to judge anyone's response and to empathize with everyone. If
people ask questions, as they often do, answers should help convey the father as
someone in struggle, trying to figure out what to do with feelings of guilt and
shame.

Examples of questions and responses are:

Q: Is your daughter okay?

A: She was fine the next day. Emotionally, I have no idea what she's thinking.
She's six.

Q: Did that change your relationship with your daughter?

A: My daughter loves me. I love her. We'll see when she's older, right?!

Q: Have you ever done anything like that again?

A: No.

Q: What did your wife do?

A: Obviously she had words with me. I've never done anything like that ever
again.

5. Generally, more people respond positively to this question.

When I was five, I thought it was funny that there was a flower called baby's breath – remember baby's breath? So I brought some to school and I was like, 'Smell this baby's breath', and the girls were like, 'Eek, no! What are we gonna do!?' Then I did the same thing with kissing. 'I'm going to kiss you.' 'Eek, no! What are we gonna do!?' And then I did the same thing with my wiener. I would pull down my pants and be like: 'I'm going to pee on you with my wiener... Patritcia.'

Who by the way, later that year, me and Patritcia were in an elevator and we touched tongues.

Anyway, 'I'm gonna pee on you with my wiener!' 'Eek, no! What am I gonna do?' 'I don't know, maybe run away from my wiener?'

And the funny thing was, that school was kindergarten to grade six. Everyone watched me do that, and nobody did anything.

Beat.

I drank pee. Remember the first time you drank pee? Mine was when I was in grade one at around six years old. I pee'd into a cup, put it in the fridge, went over to the next-door neighbour's house and said: 'Would you like some freshly squeezed lemonade?' And she was like: 'That's not lemonade'. And I was like, 'Yes, it is. See?'

He sips.

And she was like: 'That's still not lemonade'.

And I remember thinking, 'But why? I wrote lemonade on the cup, and I put a straw in it. Maybe it's because I said it was freshly squeezed and it had no pulp.'

But I wanted to get that girl, right? So, I did the same thing with poo. I went home, I put a baking sheet on the ground, squatted over it, took a poop, took an ice-cream scooper and made little balls, took a fork and twisted them to make it look fancy, put rainbow-coloured sprinkles on, put it in the fridge to harden, went back to the next-door neighbour's house, and said: 'Would you like some freshly made chocolate truffles?'

She was like: 'Those aren't chocolate truffles.'

And I was like: 'Yes they are. See?'

He pops a truffle into his mouth.

I don't know how many of you have tried poo? But it does not taste like it smells. It's got like… it coats your mouth… like nitrogen.

But we all have our own version of that, right?

A beat of complicity with a member of the audience.

You? Come on!

Gestures to audience member suggesting that they have jerked off, and tasted their own cum.

I see you.

Beat. Complicity. He proceeds.

When I was fifteen a bunch of us wanted to play a prank on this girl, Jennifer. She was like a loser. But she had a car.

I shouldn't say that.

It was a station wagon.

Oh we were all losers. But she was like the loser of the losers. I'm not judging. I'm just painting a picture. You know?

So, the plan was to scare the SHIT out of Jennifer by staging a break-in. And I would be hiding in a deep freeze, wearing a balaclava and when Jennifer came real close, I would jump out, she would scream… and that will be funny.

There were three girls and two guys, and it was this other girl's house and you go down these stairs into her basement, and here is this living room in the basement, then you go down a dark corridor towards the cellar, and around the corner there's a deep freeze and I'm in the deep freeze.

And in order for the plan to work, Jennifer has to be the first one to go around the corner, which makes zero sense because it's not her house, but… whatever.

So. About an hour before Jennifer comes over, we trash the basement. And this is the time before cell phones, so I have to rely on the signal, which is Amanda comes downstairs and says, 'Now. Get in the deep freeze now. We're gonna do it now!'

Then Amanda goes back upstairs, and she goes, 'Oh my god, the basement has been torn apart by robbers. We have to go back into the basement and make sure that the robbers aren't still there!' And Jennifer goes, 'Why?' And Amanda says, 'Don't be stupid, Jennifer. Come on, guys. Let's go scan the whole basement!' And everyone, including Jennifer, says, 'Yeah!'

So stupid.

Now just to be clear, there is a lot of pressure on me for this thing to work. 'Cause I'm in the deep freeze, wearing a balaclava, breathing through a crack, so I'm really hot. But I'm also cold, because I'm in a deep freeze. And there's like a frozen lamb shank, and a minced meat pie and a box of those meloné bars which are my favourite, and I'm kind of hungry, and I'm like take a bite, no don't take a bite, you have a job to do, stay focused. Right?

Anyway.

So.

They all come downstairs and everyone is screaming. And Jennifer's screaming the loudest – 'Ahhh! Noooooo!!!!' – and because Jennifer has to be the first one around the corner, they start pushing her down that dark corridor towards the deep freeze.

And I don't know how I know this but I feel like I can see Amanda pushing her going like:

'Just go, Jennifer. Just go.'

And her going, 'No. Please I don't want to.'

'Just go.'

'No. I don't want to…'

Jennifer rounds the corner, I jump out and yell: 'AHHHHH!!!'

Jennifer screams, lurches backwards, hits her head on the brick wall, falls to the ground, starts hyperventilating BECAUSE Jennifer is asthmatic! And we're like, 'Oh my god – hahaha – oh my god!' Right? Because we're scared but we're also kind of proud because the plan worked, you know? But Jennifer is really hyperventilating because she's having an asthma attack. And she's like, 'Puffer! Puffer!', and we don't know where her fucking puffer is!

We're like:
'Call the cops.'
'No don't call the cops. We'll gonna get in trouble.'
'Okay. Call an ambulance!'
'Okay!'
'Okay, Jennifer, Jennifer, we're calling you an ambulance, but you can't say that we had anything to do with this okay?'
'Okay. Puffer. Puffer.'
'Ya, ya, ya. It's on its way. Jennifer, focus. Jennifer, the story is you were coming downstairs… Jennifer – look at me! The story is you were coming downstairs to go to the bathroom and a raccoon jumped out… and…'
Jennifer passes out.

Fuck! She didn't hear the whole story.

We call the ambulance anyway, and then quickly tidy the basement. That way if Jennifer comes to and starts talking about raccoons, people will just think she's nuts. So we are totally in the clear.

But for *Jennifer*, things go from bad to worse because it turns out that she is really fucked up. And she has to go to the hospital and spend a week inside of an oxygen tent. And we go visit her. And we look at her. Through that plastic. And touch hands through that blue-tinted plastic window.

And…

I'm lying. We don't go visit her. We call her. Some of us. On day six. And she's happy to hear from us. She says: 'Thanks for calling, guys. I get it. It was funny. But one question… why did it have to be just me?'

Beat.

You know I don't even know her anymore. Like in her life. I know that she's single. Still. And I know she has her own catering company called Niceties. Spelled, Nice-EATies. For real. Kind of makes you want to barf or punch her. And maybe I interviewed her to be the caterer for my wedding… but I didn't go with her… because I didn't like her style… as usual.

Later my wife asked me, 'How could you call her after all that?'

I thought we'd get a deal!

Points at someone in the audience.

You know what I mean.

Beat. He proceeds.

I feel like I should tell you how I lost my virginity now. It wasn't with Jennifer. Cool your jets. I was bad. Or fine. It was fast. Or awkward. I kept yelling: 'It's so moist!'

Shakes his head as if to confirm that he was a loser and 'knew no better'.

I had so much porn on my computer. Man, at one point, I had so much porn on my computer that I thought I might get arrested if the wrong person got a hold of my hard drive on the wrong day. Not because of anything kiddie… nothing like that. Just the mass amounts of pics and gifs. No videos. 'Cause this was the early days of the internet. Like I don't know what you people do. And by you people, I mean, like, your generation… For you it's like – *BAM* – it's just there. For us, it was like twenty-five seconds per pic. Like: tick tick tick tick. Suspension. Tension. Tits. It was time-consuming.

And special. So, I saved everything on to my hard drive and then, buried the evidence in folders within subfolders, within subdrives, so the cops wouldn't find me.

For example: my computer, C-drive, documents, movies, comedies, satires, political satires, eighties satires, eighties political satires, fun times, pics. And just to be clear, nothing was in any of those folders until you get to pics. And then when you open pics, it's celebrities and porn stars, A–Z, pics and gifs. For example: pics – 'J' – celebrities, pics, 'Jennifer Aniston's tits running away from guy dot jpg.' And it was great 'cause I could watch Jennifer Aniston's tits and didn't have to watch her shitty movie.

Or 'S': Sandra Bullock, full exposure, going incognito, in the airport washroom, trying to escape the Russian spies. Escape on my dick! Yeah!

Oh I know that's gross. But that's the mind of a sixteen to twenty-five to eighty-seven-year-old man. Escape on my dick! Yeeeeeah! Sandra. Sandra's tits.

Tit's Congeniality.
Mary Poptits.
The Tit, the Tit and the Wardrobe.
Schindler's Tit? I could have saved one more…!
Tit's a Wonderful Life.
Titanator Two: Judgment Tit.

Man, being a dad is hard. You can't tell jokes like that anymore.

Points to someone in the audience.

But we'll try.

Back to the subfolders: porn, bondage, black, brown, blonde, brunette, redhead, unique. Orgies, backyard parties, food porn, fetish porn, tit porn, furry porn, pierced nipples, Russian maids. There was one pic of a swirly shit going into this girl's mouth. And I give you that image, so you can have in your mind what I have in my mind. Forever. I didn't like it. They seemed happy.

That went under 'D': disturbing, pics.

I lied before when I said I didn't have any videos. I had like one. Or five. D: disturbing, vids. There was this one sixty second clip of a horse fucking a woman on a ranch. Do you know that one? It's a classic. There was a haystack, she's got pigtails, and the hat. And she's leaning over the haystack and the horse is over her and she makes that sound and… I'll just do it.

Does sound – a woman yelling in sharp unrelenting staccato bursts.

Blech. I did not like it.

But I kept it to remind myself what I *wasn't* into: bestiality – or as my mom likes to call it, '*best*-iality' – feces, and fisting. Like if that's your thing, totally cool, no judgment. Just not my thing.

Back to my subfolders. Outdoors, office buildings, rooftops, aging, extreme sports, felching, welding, smelting, gangbang whores… aging gangbang whores, aging rooftop gangbang whores who smelt… whilst welding. Bruising, needles, cutting.

Just kidding. That's a little bit too far. Right?

But you're okay with smelting, aging gangbang whores.

Great.

So that happened.

Gesture of sweeping under a rug.

Beat. He proceeds.

In my twenties, I went to Japan. It was unlike anything I've ever been to. I loved it. Legend has it that when young western men go to Japan they are worshipped by Japanese women. And I felt it the moment I got on the plane to go. I remember sitting in a seat in between three women, or in a position where I shouldn't have been served first, and the stewardess came up to us and served me first. And I thought: I like this! For the first time in my life, I felt privilege.

I don't mean that kind of privilege. Of course I have privilege – I'm a middleclass Jew who went to summer camp. I'm aware this was like I was handed the privilege of kings. In the land of the geisha, I would have one. Girls called me David Beckham, and I was like, 'No! I'm not David Beckham. I don't have blonde hair.' And they were like, 'Okay. You are Ben Affleck.' And I was like, 'Okay! I'm Ben Affleck.'

And this was the time of *Good Will Hunting*.

Japan was nuts!

They don't actually have geisha anymore. But what they do have is vending machines where you can buy used women's panties to like smell, or wear, or I don't know, eat, I guess.

They also have these salarymen, which are like businessman in suits, on the Metro, reading hardcore Japanese porn manga in front of everyone. Like children and families are watching.

I was taken to one club where you go to fuck air. Like, you go in and everyone's standing around, listening to J-Pop, fucking air. And when you get turned on enough, you go into these private booths in the back where they have Kleenex and Wet-Ones, and you finish.

They took me to another club where you would sit in a reclining chair and order a drink from someone dressed as Sailor Moon or a nurse, or a unicorn – you choose the costume from a menu – and they bring you your Manhattan, and you lean back, and gaze up through a glass ceiling where there are panty-less women dancing for your pleasure. Like dancing vaginas. Hello Kitty. It was awesome!

And the thing about Japan was, you do those things, you wake up the next day and nobody talks about it. It's over. It's weird.

When I came back to Canada, I brought home a ton of gifts for my friends and loved ones, including for my two best guy friends, a couple VHS tapes of Japanese porn. Because I thought it would be funny.

And the reason I thought it would be funny is because in Japanese porno, they blur out the genitals. And, they also just fuck. There's no storyline. There's no porno version of *Jurassic Park*. You know, *Your Ass Has Had It Park, Part II: Back to Backdoor Island*. You know that one?

'Oh no! There's a velociraptor.'
'Quick, get in the bush and fuck me in the ass.'
'That solved the problem. Phew!'

I like that kind. Japanese porn is weird because it's just happening.

So I present my friends the tapes and I haven't watched them yet. I just picked them based on the title and it's one of these orgy or gangbang scenarios. Which I still don't know the difference between. Does anyone here know the difference? Between an orgy and a gangbang?

He has a discussion with the audience to figure out the difference.[6]

Alright. We'll leave it there for tonight. Thank you so much for your participation.

So we put on the movie. And first thing we notice is, it's really well lit. And then these two guys walk in, and they're like, 'Ohayo gozaimashita. Ohayo gozaimashita.' And they take off their clothes and fold them very neatly and put them in the corner out of the way. And then this girl comes in from over here and she says, 'Ohayo gozaimashita.' And lies down on the floor, nude. And this guy says to his friend: 'I'm going to finger her.'

And he does.

---

6. As with the earlier audience interaction about violence, it is necessary to listen and empathize. It's not necessary to receive a correct definition. You just want them speaking. Some suggested responses and prompts:

Does anyone else agree?

Does anyone have a different thought?

Does anyone want to add anything we haven't thought of?

Often someone immediately responds by saying: consent. Suggested responses are:

Even in a movie?

Does anyone agree or have a different thought?

If an audience member speaks about binary orgies or gangbangs, challenge that idea.

And remember, because of the blurred-out genitals, this is what you see –

He mimes.

Blurry, not-blurry, blurry, not-blurry.

And it's weird and stupid and kind of boring, because only the men are talking, and the women are just yelling. The women they make this sound. It's confusing. Is it pleasure or is it pain? Even if they're only just kissing, the women are yelling.

And I was just having this conversation the other day with my friends. So, I looked up a clip online – and I put it on my phone.

Hold on.

I put it on my phone, and then buried the evidence. Because I didn't want my wife or my daughter to find it. So I put it under a playlist called 'J-pop plus'.

See? J pop-plus. Because they don't like J-pop. Which is weird.

Here. Listen.

Plays soundtrack to a Japanese porno film where the woman is very verbal.

See? Is that pleasure or is that pain? It's confusing. And see? He's talking. And I gotta say I feel like she's a bad actress. Like pick an intention, and go with it so I know how to feel about what you're doing, right? Like that velociraptor lady, you know? She is so clear.

Anyway.

Picks up porn mime.

So, this keeps happening for a bit and it's weird, stupid and boring and then things take a turn as this guy pulls out, she visibly relaxes, he walks away and says to one of his buddies: 'See? I just fingered her,' and this guy says: 'Oh, she's not done.' And then he comes back over to her and really starts going at it. Like this.

The mime becomes aggressive.

And then my friends and I start feeling uncomfortable, kind of cramping up because we feel like we're watching a rape. And she is yelling. Very intensely. And then he pulls out and there's this massive wad, and he goes – (*Flick fingers with sound of viscosity.*) And she goes, 'AHHHH!'

And WE. ARE. DONE.

We turn it off.

And when my friends leave, I turn it back on.

A long beat. He stands tall. Nods. Defends. He proceeds.

I've done a lot of bad shit. Like thinking it was a good idea to live across the street from Fillmore's Gentlemen's Club in my 'dirty thirties'. You know that place? It's an iconic downtown Toronto strip club. And like that whole scene.

Mimes opening the doors to Fillmore's and air drums Phil Collins' 'In the Air Tonight'.

I can feel it coming – All that neon – *tonight*. Hold on… Right?

And the girls are smokin' hot. And if you go on a Sunday there's this Montreal Bagel buffet – great spread. And like you eat your bagel and watch the strippers do the pole and you kinda feel sorry for her because she has to work the bagel shift. And you can get a lap dance in the back for twenty bucks a song. And they shorten the songs. And then at the three-quarter mark, the girls start to appreciate you like: 'Your brain is so big, and your thighs are so strong.' And I'm like: 'Okay!'

Mimes handing over money.

I slept with three – five hookers in my time.

And it was bad. Like on my part. Like what was I thinking? I was thinking they liked me!

Mimes handing over money.

So, naturally, during those days, I contracted a couple of non-life-threatening STDs. But who hasn't, right?

But nothing serious. Like HPV and... if you're happy and you know it: *hmm, hmm, hmm...*

Claps a few times.

And I keep sleeping around, probably spreading my jam, and I don't tell any of the women about it. And I know a lot of guys with that story. Like who here has cold sores, right?

Hands up.

Lights up.

Just kidding.

Hands down.

The STDs aren't that bad. And I do call each one of those women eventually, and I profusely apologize, and they yell at me and I take it. I totally take it.

When I got married I told my wife about the STDs. Not *when* we got married. Could you imagine?

I do! I do too!

(He sings.) Hava nagila – I've got gonorrhea.

No.

But when we get married – I stop sleeping with hookers. I declare it and that's it.

And the last one is fucking awesome. It's sweaty, and contorted, and durational. She keeps her heels on. I had one of those bars above my door frame. And we took turns swinging and being on and with, everything.

And when she left, I went out onto my little balcony, and under the bright neon lights of Fillmore's Gentleman's Club, I smoked the last cigarette I would ever smoke.

He wants to go back to the party.

That time was wild.

I have these fantasies of going back there and being let off the hook. I love my family, but I just want three days.

He reaches for his music player and finds the perfect song.

I want to go to a club...

Plays a music track à la Peaches' 'AAXXX'.

I want to dance, I want to fuck, I want to fuck air, I want to do coke, I want to do coke off the air, I want to eat cake, I want to drink, I want to puke, I want to pass out, I want to wake up... and I wanna do it all again.

He drinks from the water glass, finishing it in a few boozed-up gulps. Still holding the glass, he retreats in the space, into the shadows. He is watching the audience. Seducing them and challenging them to be complicit in the moment. He advances, looks up to the heavens, opens up and a fountain of mist pours from his mouth. It's sensual and disgusting.

He returns to the music player and turns it off. He takes the pink bandana and mops himself dry.

Isn't that familiar?

Silence.

I've had two affairs. The first one isn't really worth talking about. The second is with a sixteen-year-old.

Which by the way is the legal age of consent in Canada. Some people think it's eighteen, but it's not. It's sixteen. Some people think that it's fourteen, but it's not. That's the two-year rule. In Canada, a fourteen-year-old can sleep with a sixteen-year-old, not a seventeen-year-old, a fifteen-year-old can sleep with seventeen-year-old, not an eighteen-year-old. Eighteen is the legal age of consent in Canada for anal.

I think.

I should check.

So, I meet the sixteen-year-old at a bat mitzvah. And to be clear, it wasn't her bat mitzvah. She's the bat mitzvah girl's older cousin.

And we start this crazy affair. And she invites me to these parties with all of these teenagers and college kids and me! I am that guy! Who would say no? Right? And these parties are fun! And we're like, hanging out, and hooking up, and doing drugs. Like PCP. Have you ever done PCP? It's like:

He verbalizes the ecstatic soundscape of being high on PCP:

'Yeow… Mlurb… Welcome…'

It's fucking awesome. Like I don't even know if you can get it anymore, but if you can, call a friend or a 'dealer', I have no connections anymore, but do yourself a favour and try it once in your life. At least.

So this one night, we go to this party and we're so fucked up and we go into this back room and we're fucking and so high, and she says: 'Hit me.'

And I'm like: 'I'm not into that.'
And she's like: 'Do it.'

So I do it. Lightly.

And then she says: 'Is that all you got, pussy?'
Like that's gonna work.
And then she goes, 'Don't be afraid, little boy.'

Beat.

'Let's go. Do it.'

Beat.

He mimes punching her.

Sound and lights are called.

Suddenly, the play takes a hard turn as the stage, for the first time since the show began, is supported by theatrical elements. The sound of the punch is loud, and the stage is lit to express.

From this moment onward, the text of the play is heightened, and no longer casual in delivery.

The 'play' has begun.

The sound and lighting design continue to grow and intensify for the remainder of the play, building to a climax in the play's final moments.

And I break her eye-socket.

Silence.

And she says, 'I'm so sorry, that was my fault.'

Silence.

That is so fucked up. Who thinks like that?

She was going to do it to herself. There was a hammer there. She was eyeing the bedpost. The girl was looking for violence. And I rose to the occasion.

Alice.

Beat.

Affairs are hard. My wife was amazing. I went to therapy. I hiked the Camino trail. I had a daughter.

And then we had a holiday party. Twenty people, adults in the kitchen, my kids and their friends in the basement. Except for ten-year-old Ryan who stays upstairs in the living room alone watching TV, 'cause Ryan's a fuckin' wimp. You graze this kid and he runs to his dad Peter, bawling. He is a loser. And that one's on Peter: 'You okay, Ry-ry? Is it ouchy?' Come on! Teach your ten-year-old *son* to grow a pair. I have a daughter. I am scared all the time. Is *she* going to be okay?

You know that joke? How do you make a hormone? Stick a rusty fucking chainsaw up her twat. That's what they say about girls.

Ry-an is going to be fi-an.

My daughter, she comes upstairs for a meatball or

something, and she sees Ryan in the living room on the couch watching *My Little Pony*. So she goes in there and starts asking him:

'Aren't the flying ones pretty, Ry-ry?'
'I don't like them!', he says.
'What about the purple unicorn, Ry-ry?'
'Stop it. I don't even like this show!'

And he goes to change the channel, and my daughter grabs the remote and calls him a pony dink. I taught her that.

And Ryan starts a-cryin'.

Suddenly, they're in this intense tug-of-war over the remote. And to get some leverage, my daughter puts her foot on Ryan's face and starts tugging. And Ryan lets out a long high-pitched squeal, like a little girl, and all the adults come rushing in, and Peter and I get in front to see what's going on. And I gotta say that I like what's happening here because my daughter is defending herself and she is winning. But Peter does not like this one bit. He doesn't think it's appropriate that my daughter call his son a pony dink. His son is sensitive. My daughter should cool it.

'Stop it!' he yells.

And my daughter looks at me and I look at my daughter and I smile, and she smiles back. And Peter loses his mind. He grabs my little girl and says, 'GET OFF MY SON YOU LITTLE BITCH!' and throws her on the ground and as she hits, you hear *snap*.

When I hear that snap, my vision becomes clear and focused. I beeline for Peter, I step over my daughter, grab a fireplace poker and with the blunt end:

He mimes three hits. They are accompanied by sound and light.

'Fucker! You touch my little girl like that?!'

Beat.

People leave pretty quick. Peter doesn't press charges.

What's he gonna do? I scare my daughter though. She's over there in the corner holding her wrist. She won't let me touch her. And it takes us forty minutes to get her into the car to go the hospital. Not because she's in pain. Because I scared her so badly.

She's looking at me like I'm a monster. The same way she looked at me when I threw her into the bed that night.

And for a fucking month she won't look at me. She's got this look. I've seen it before. I recognize it. Not because of anything like this. She gets it every time she says I've upset or confused her. This gummy look... I can't reach her.

A month of silence. Imagine a house that doesn't speak, sleeping on the couch, not putting my kids to bed. My wife says, 'You do one more thing. One more thing like that. I leave you.' And I don't know how to do... anything. I'm not good at this.

And I think, talk to your daughter. So I call her in the room and I say:

He sees his daughter in space and begins to speak to her.

'Sweetheart... Sweetheart. No more. I know Daddy went a little too far but everything I do, I do it for you. Do you understand? Stop this. Please. Hey! There you are. There *we* are.

Why don't we have a dance party?

Anything you want.

You choose.

You lead. I follow.'

He sees his daughter walk over to the music player. She hesitates and eventually hits play. Carly Rae Jepsen's 'Good Time' plays. She dances around him, never with him. She evades him, moves quickly and for herself. She exits alone. The music stops.

I don't understand her.

My daughter was born with her eyes open taking in the world. And the doctors handed her to *me first* and we locked eyes for what felt like an hour. And we made a deal: I am the father, you are my daughter and I will not apologize for protecting you.

My son, he does this thing where he walks into walls on purpose because he thinks it's funny and it is. He's stalky. He's got a pot belly. Kind of built like a rugby player. But at three. And he does this: 'Oww. Oww. Oww.'

It's so simple.

This is not.

This is confusing.

She is confusing.

It's like she holds more in her head than I can.

It's mean.

It's not fair.

It's stupid.

Beat.

There's this guy from the neighbourhood whose son has the same name as mine and the last time I saw him his wife was thirty-seven weeks pregnant with a little girl. And I ran into him around the due date and I said:

'Hey, how'd it go?'

He shook his head.

'Oh. Not yet?'

'We lost the baby.'

And my first thought was, 'Well, you sure dodged a bullet. At least you didn't have to have a girl.'

What can I possibly say after I thought that?

So all I say is, 'Oh man, I am so sorry.'

But I thought that. I know it's terrible. But it's true. I still think that. His life will be simpler because he doesn't have to have a daughter. I know mine would be.

And I love her.

So what am I supposed to do with that? And when I try and work it out I go back over all of these moments and I think... well you're being a cunt.

And I guess I shouldn't say that.

But I mean it. I desperately mean it. I love my daughter. And she's being a cunt.

You know what I mean. You know exactly what I'm talking about.

And I know that it's not even at its peak yet. That it's growing and growing all the time. And I just want to push it down and make it simple again. All those cunts. Stop cunting in my face with your cunting behaviour.

What? Am I not allowed to say that? Aren't I here to share with you exactly what I'm actually thinking and feeling so that we begin move forward?

Let's get back to something simple.
You know what's simple?
Two things.
One: tits.
And two: tits.

Let's remove the cunt people and just be a room full of tits. Like how many tits do we have here tonight?

He points at the women in the audience and begins to count.

Two. Four. Eight. Twenty-four. Sixty-three. Two hundred and twenty tits![7]

This is our story. I'll be part of that too!

He unzips his hoodie, pulls down his shirt and shows his bare chest. He squeezes his pecs together to look like a pair of breasts.

---

7. Depending on the house count for each performance, the final number should represent just over half the audience.

What do you need from me? Whatever you need from me
I will do IT here tonight! I will bang it out. Make it happen.
Yeah! That's what I'm fucking talking about.

THE FATHER*'s rant ensues as sound and lights swell. He
slowly retreats upstage. His language and movement
becoming increasingly more violent.*[8] *He is breaking apart.
The sound reaches an almost deafening crescendo. The lights
turn on the audience, blinding them.* THE FATHER
disappears.

Blackout.

Sound out.

Silence.

FIN.

---

8. As the sound becomes quite loud quite quickly, the following text has never
been audible to the audience but is delivered under the cue:

Bang it out. One at a time. Apparently, every decision I make is with my dick in
my hand. So, let's do it. Lay it down motherfucker! We can start a band. Rock
hard. Just take it off! Whip 'em out. Slap 'em around a little bit. Now come at
me. Do it!